# Mother Fucker

## A Curse Word Adult Coloring Book For Release Stress

By

**S.B. Nozaz**

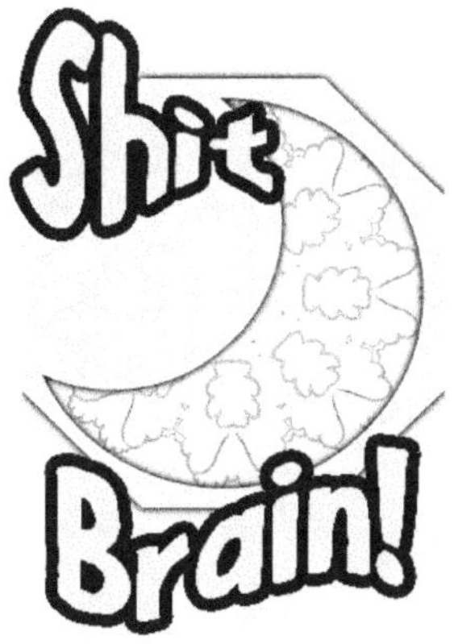

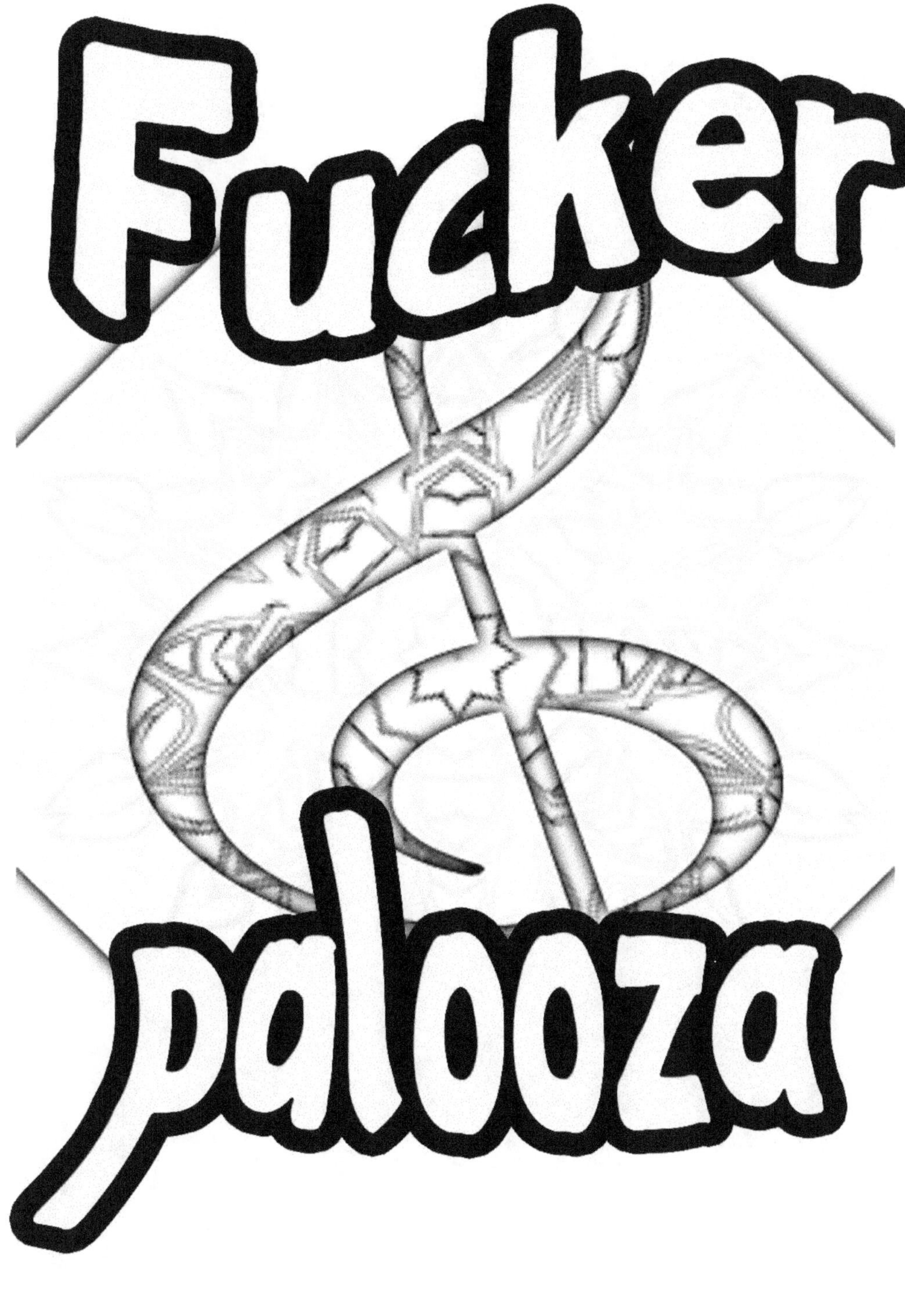
Fucker
palooza

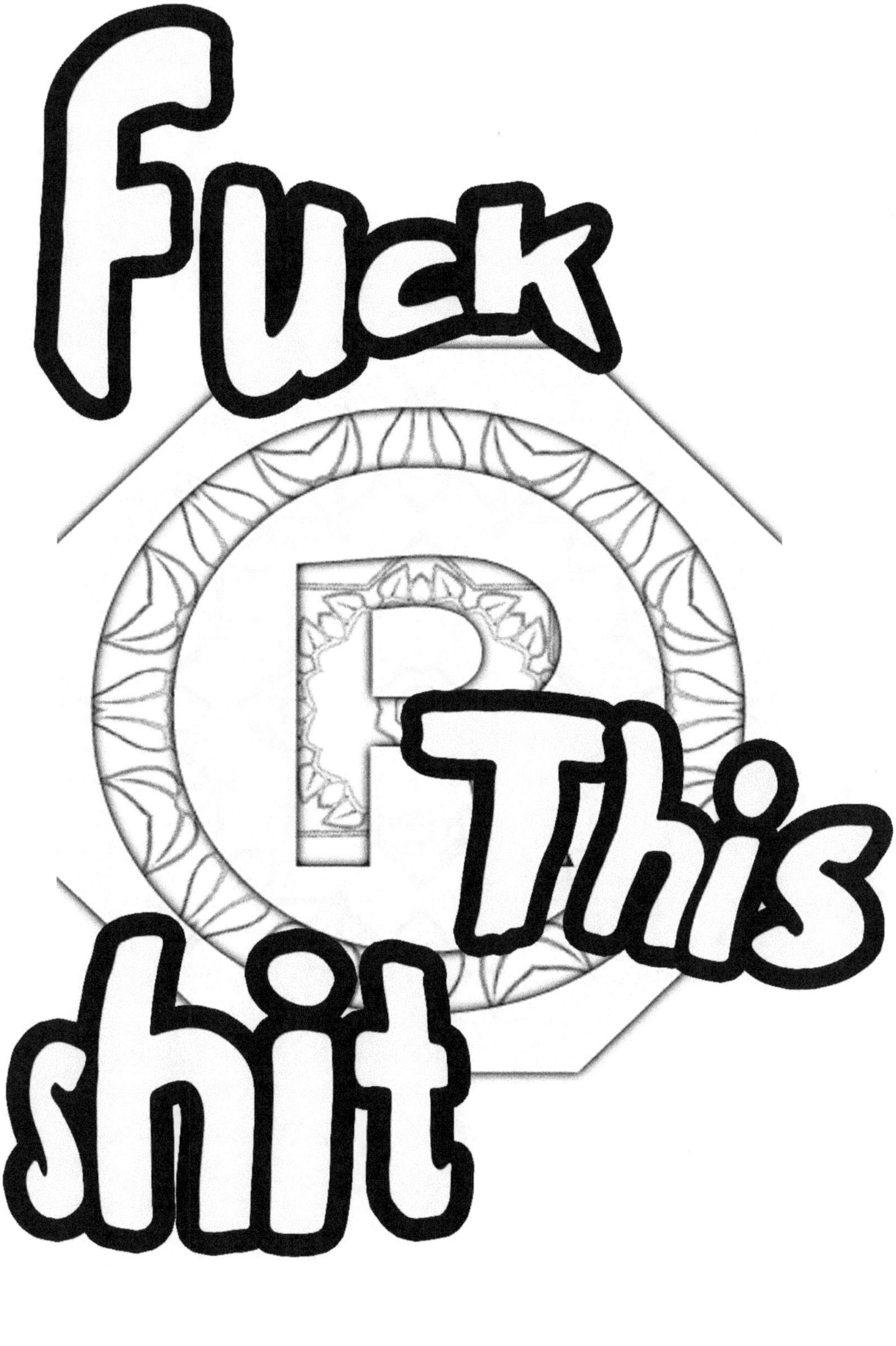
Fuck
This
shit

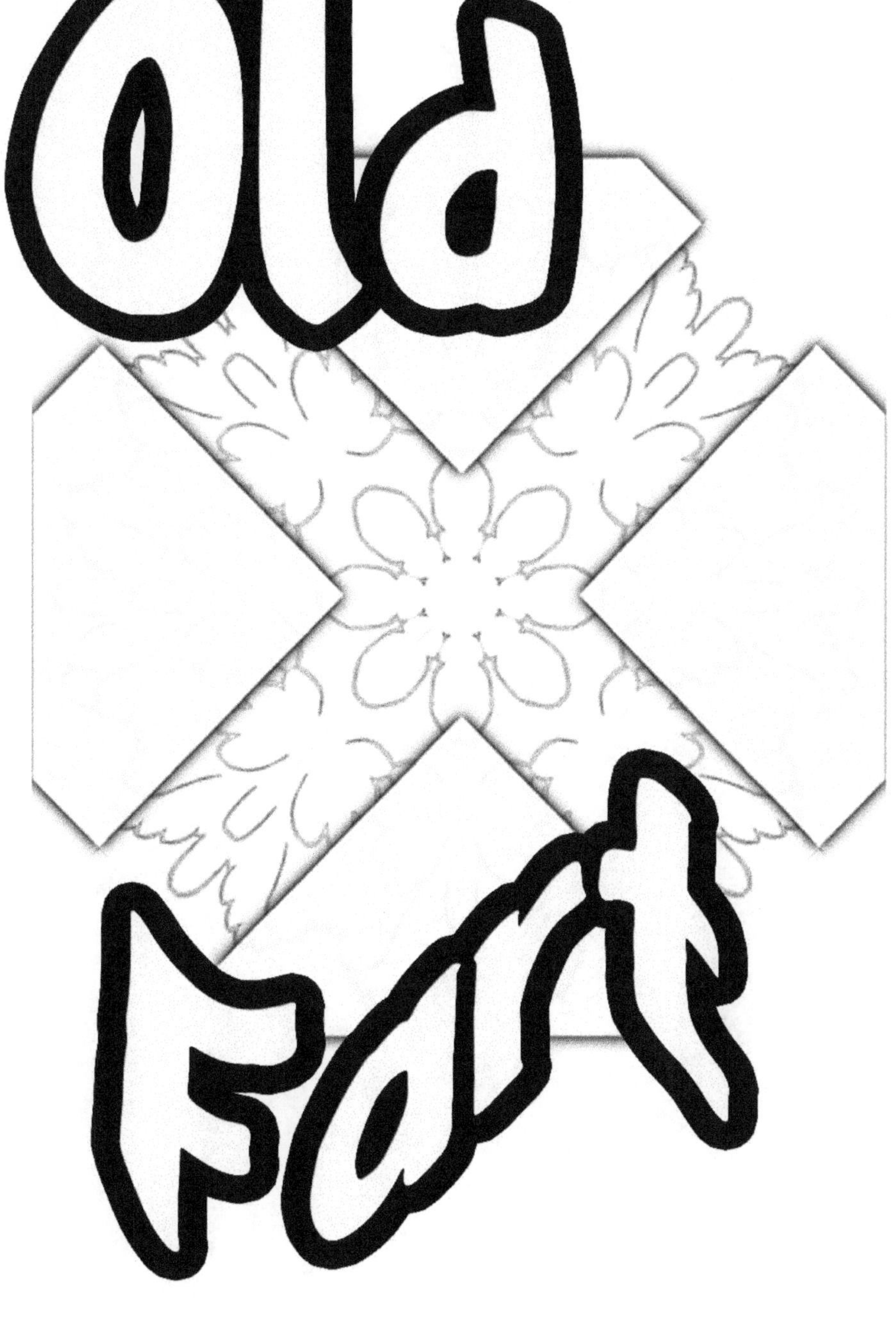
Old
Fart

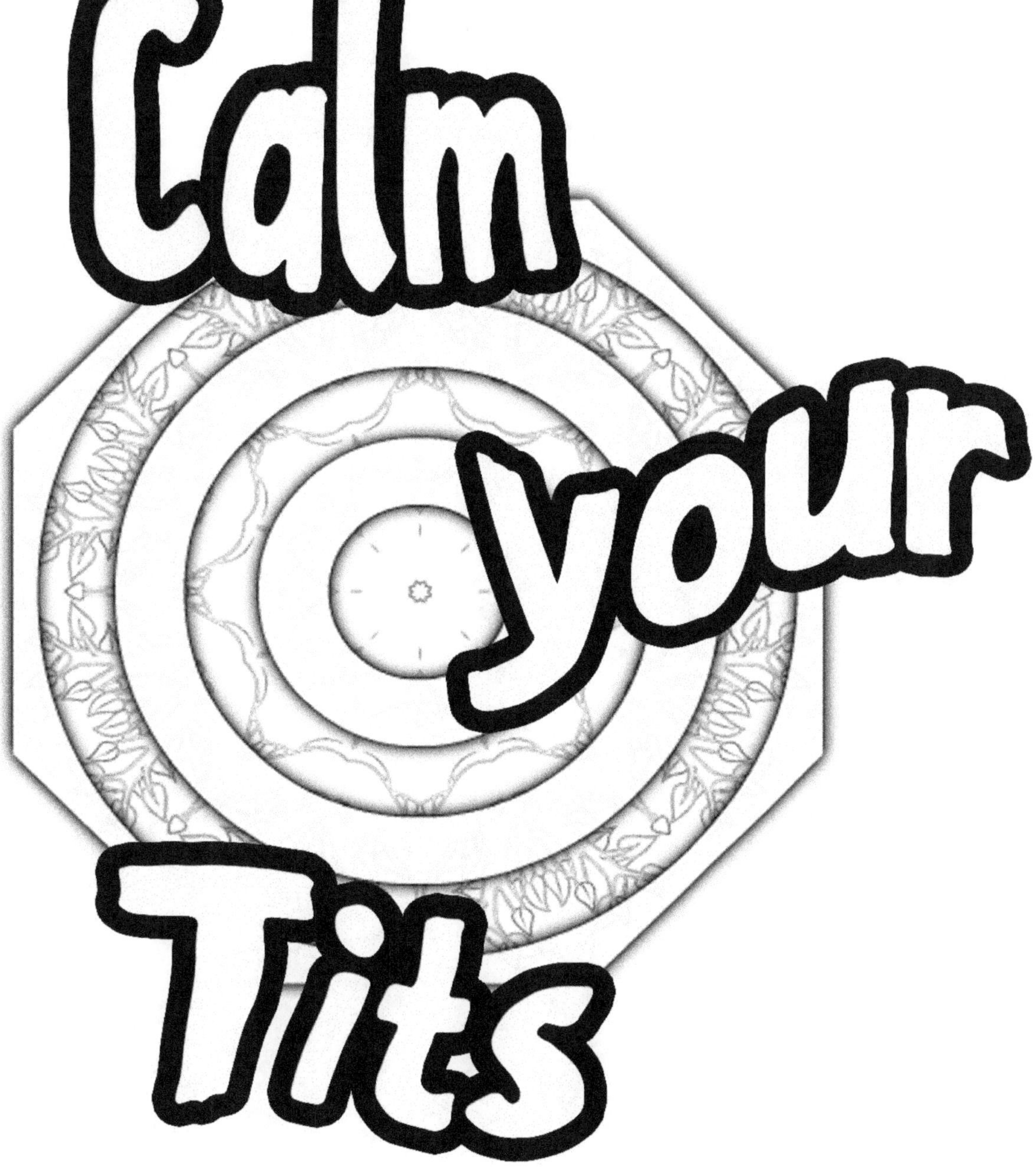
Calm
your
Tits

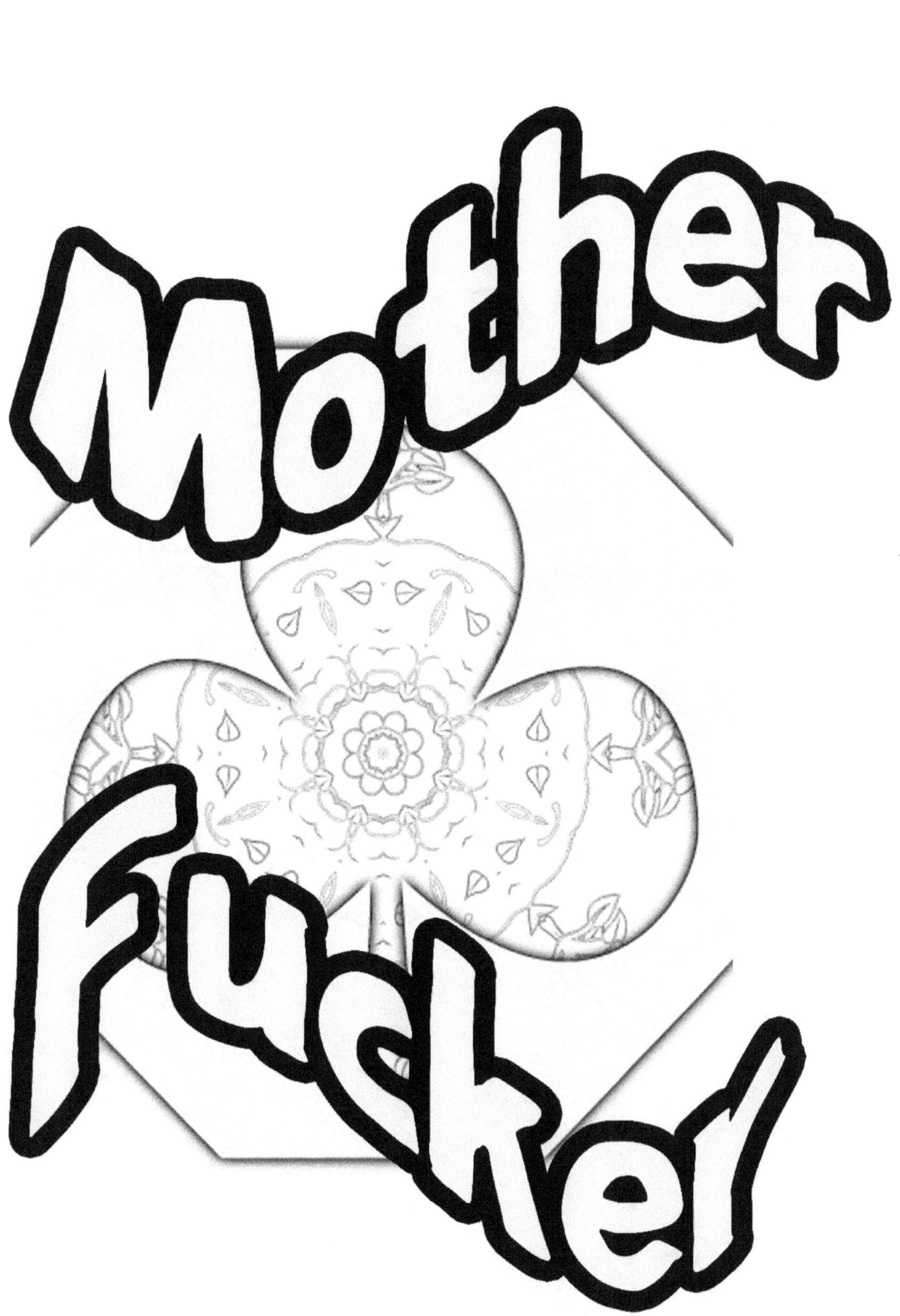
Mother
Fucker

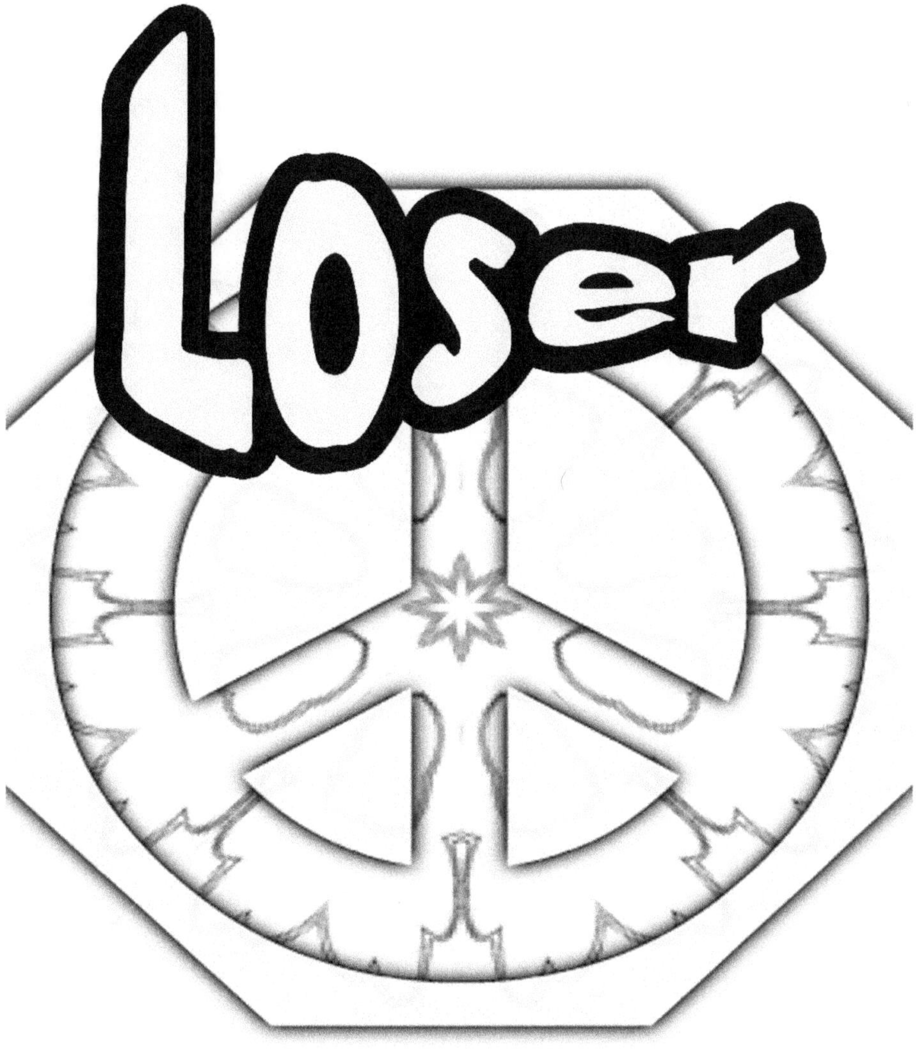
Loser

# Shitballs

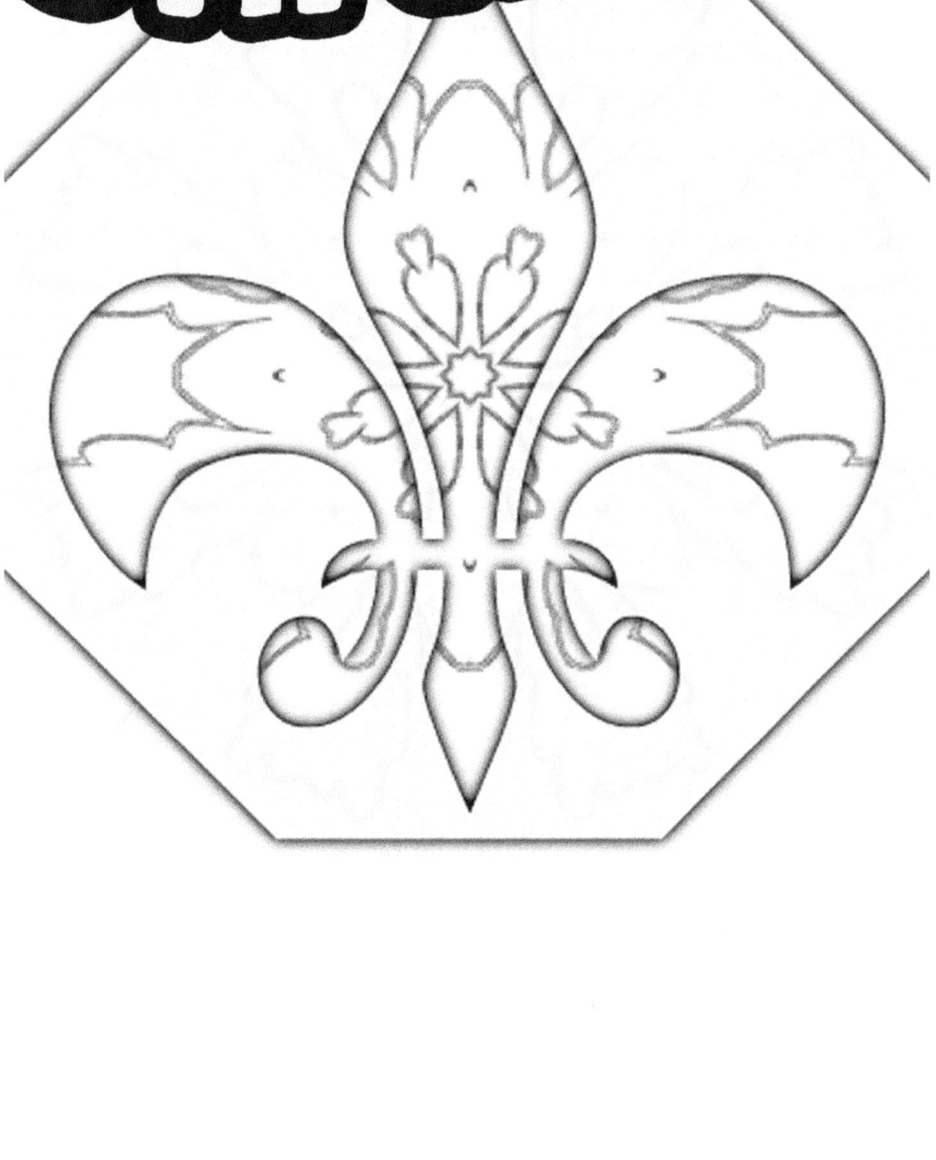

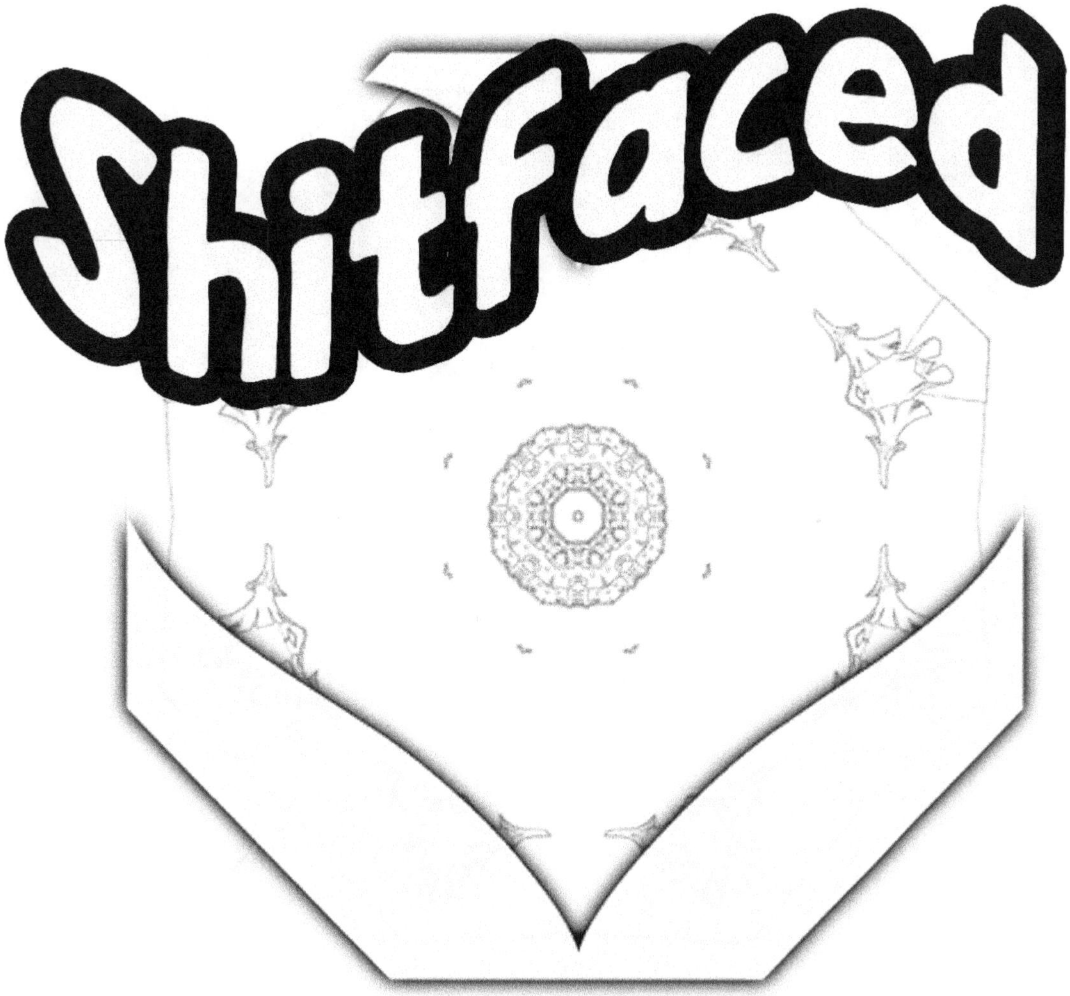
Shitfaced

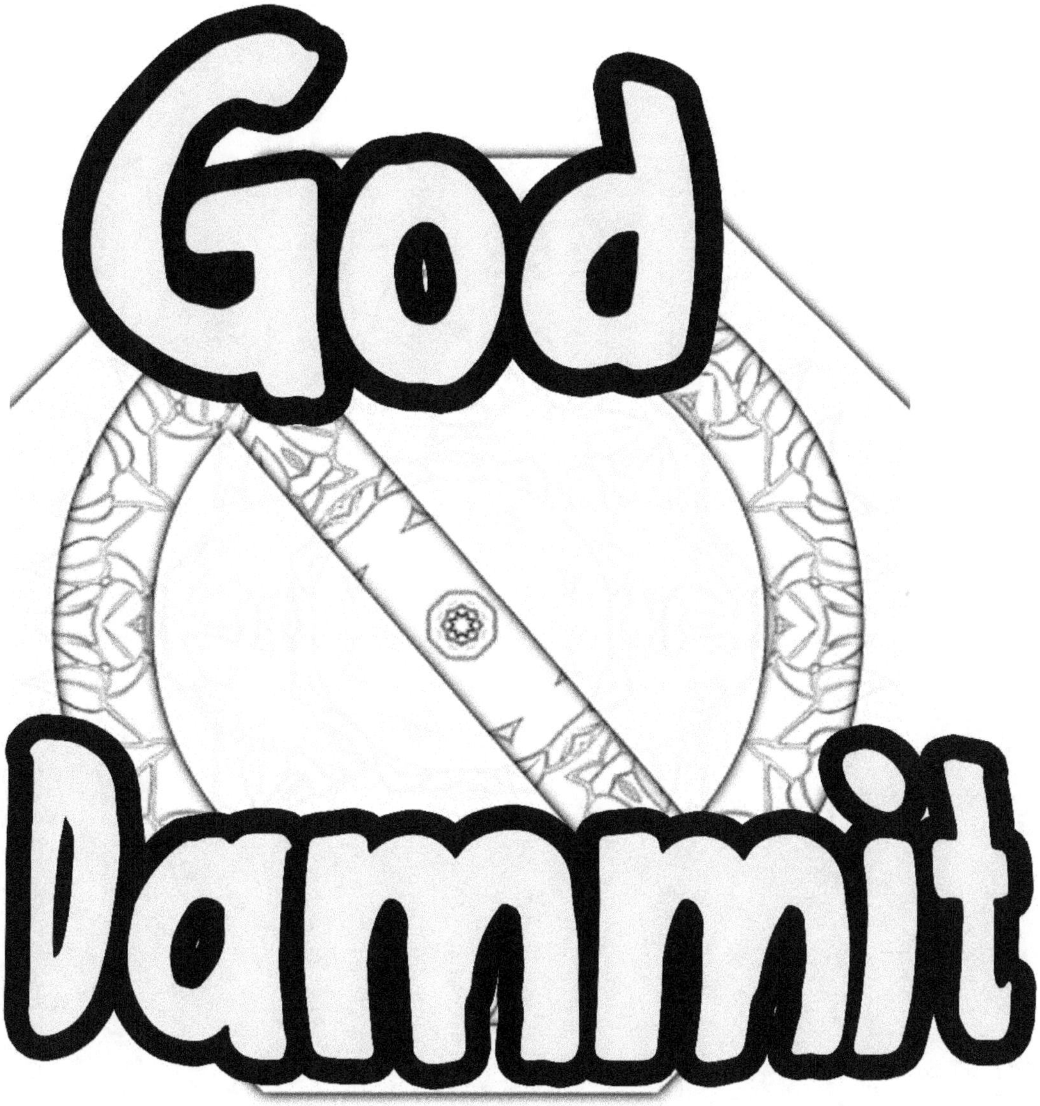
God
Dammit

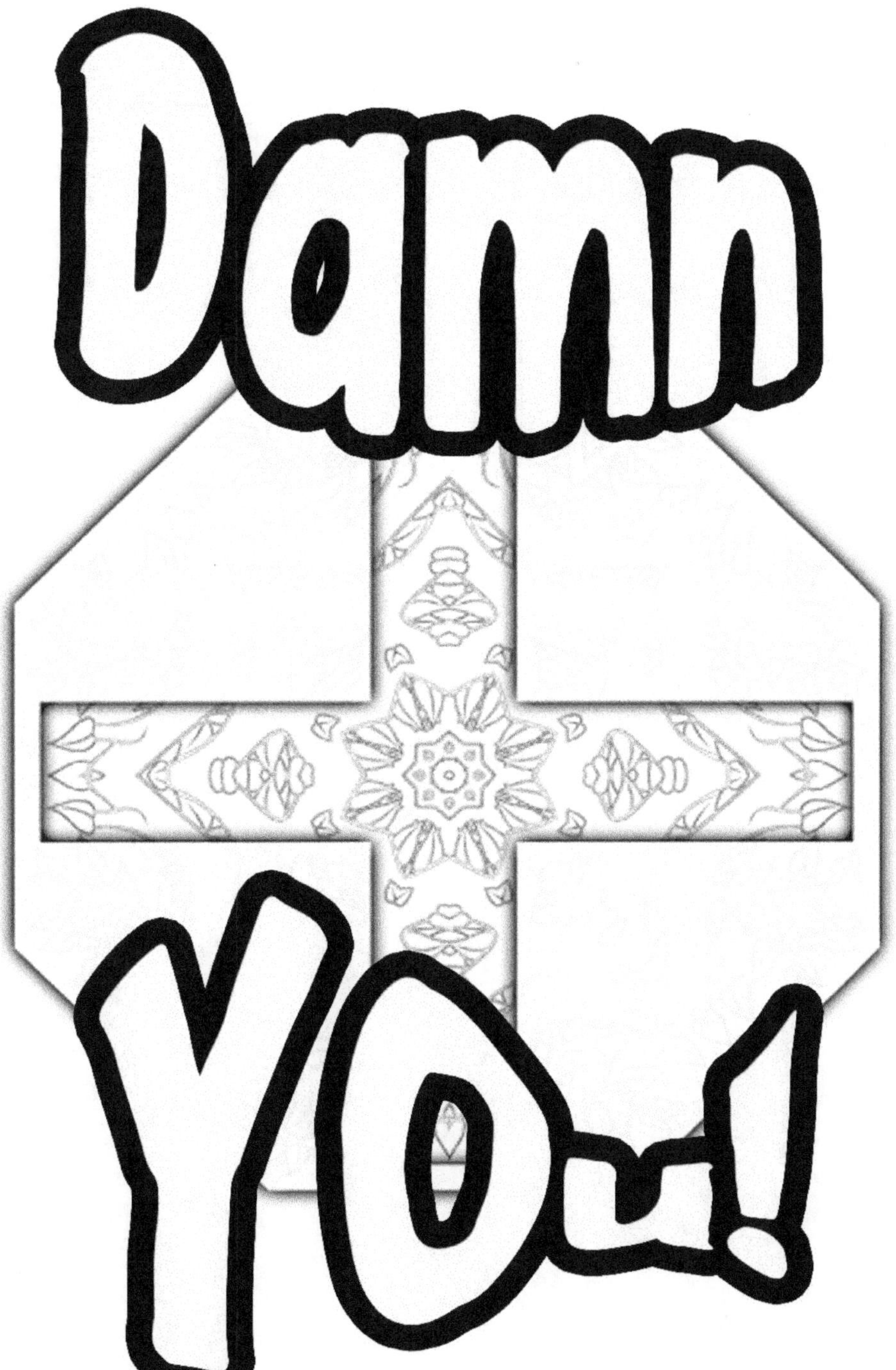
Damn
YOu!

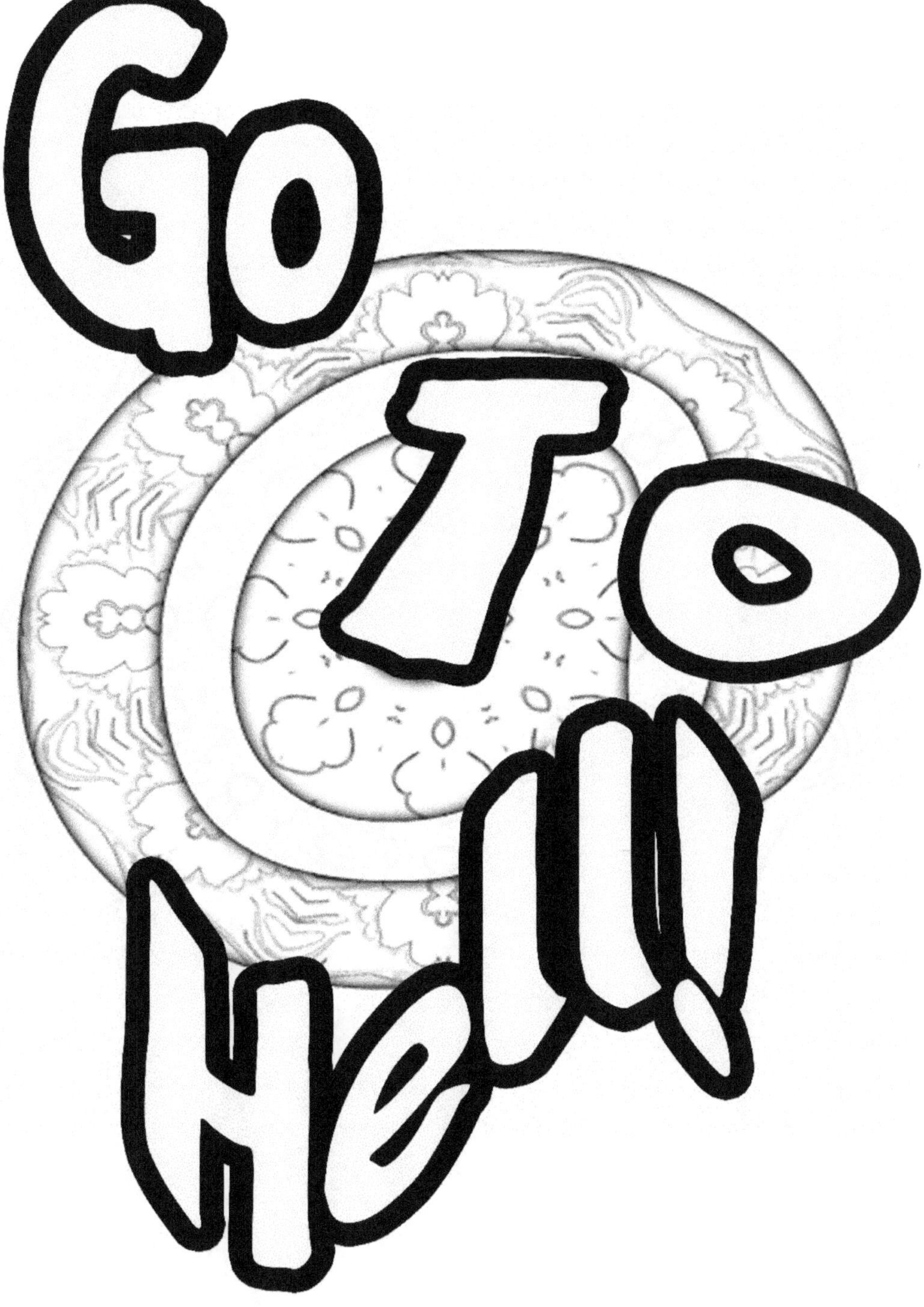
Go To Hell!

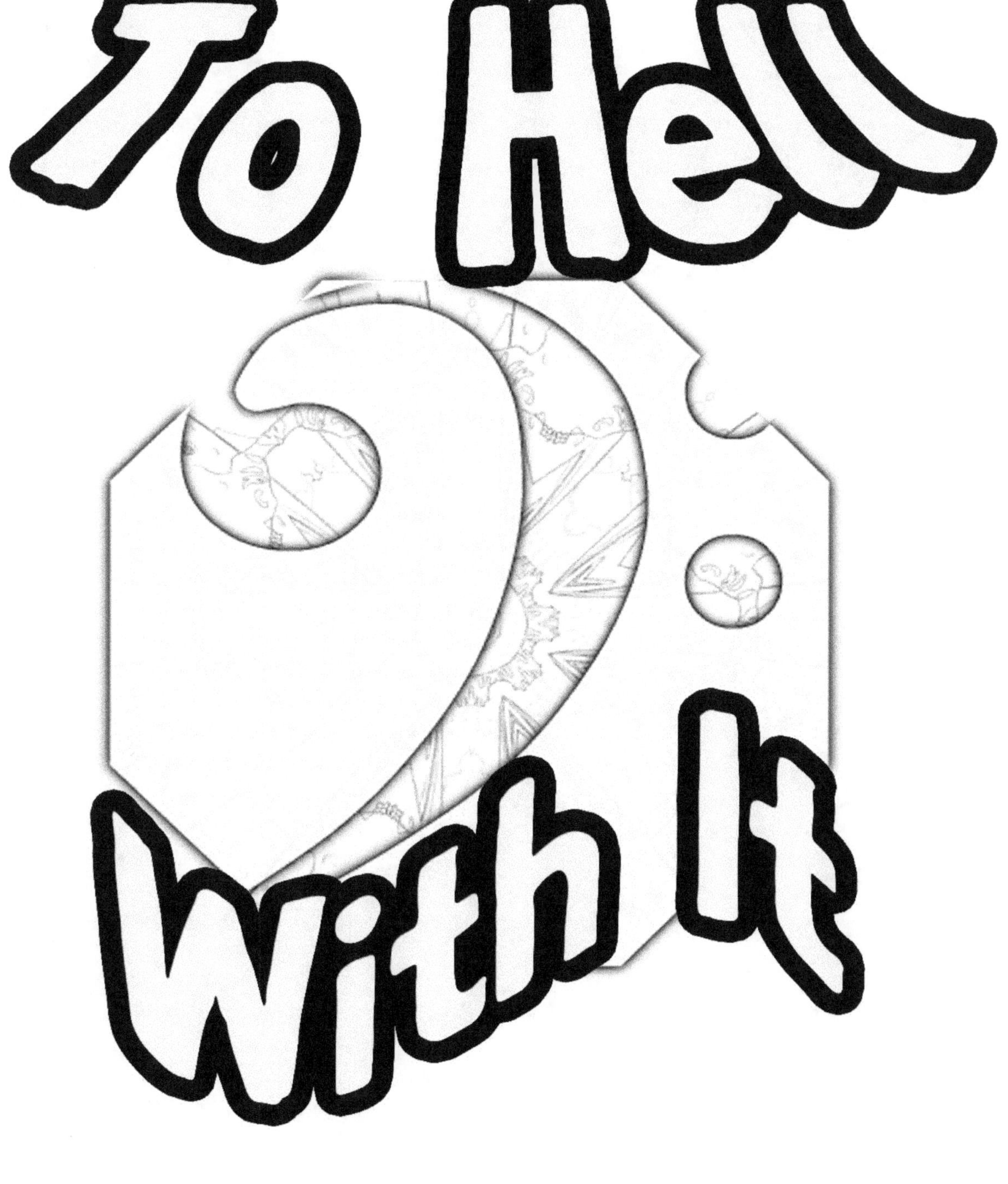
To Hell
With It

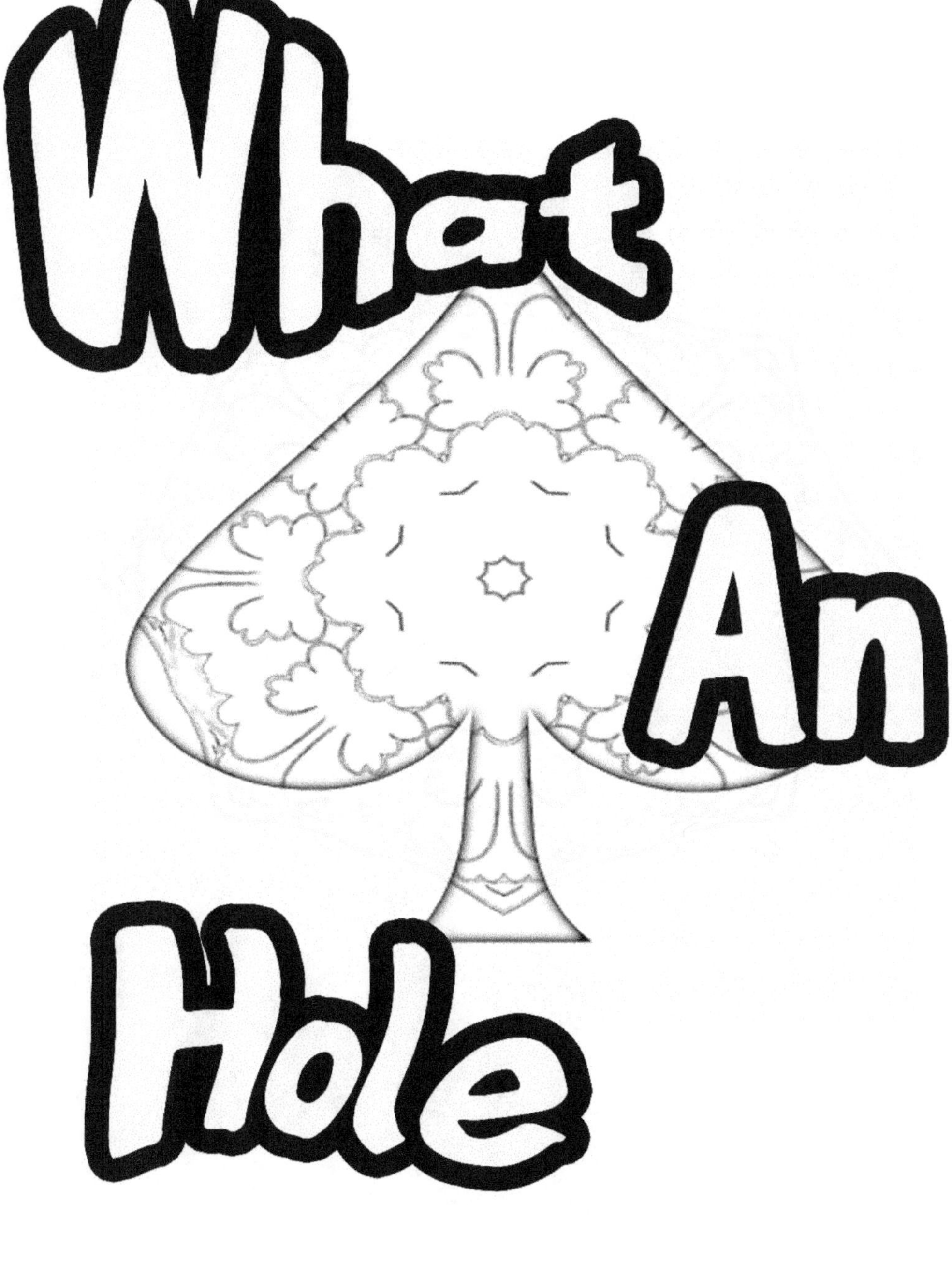
What
An
Hole

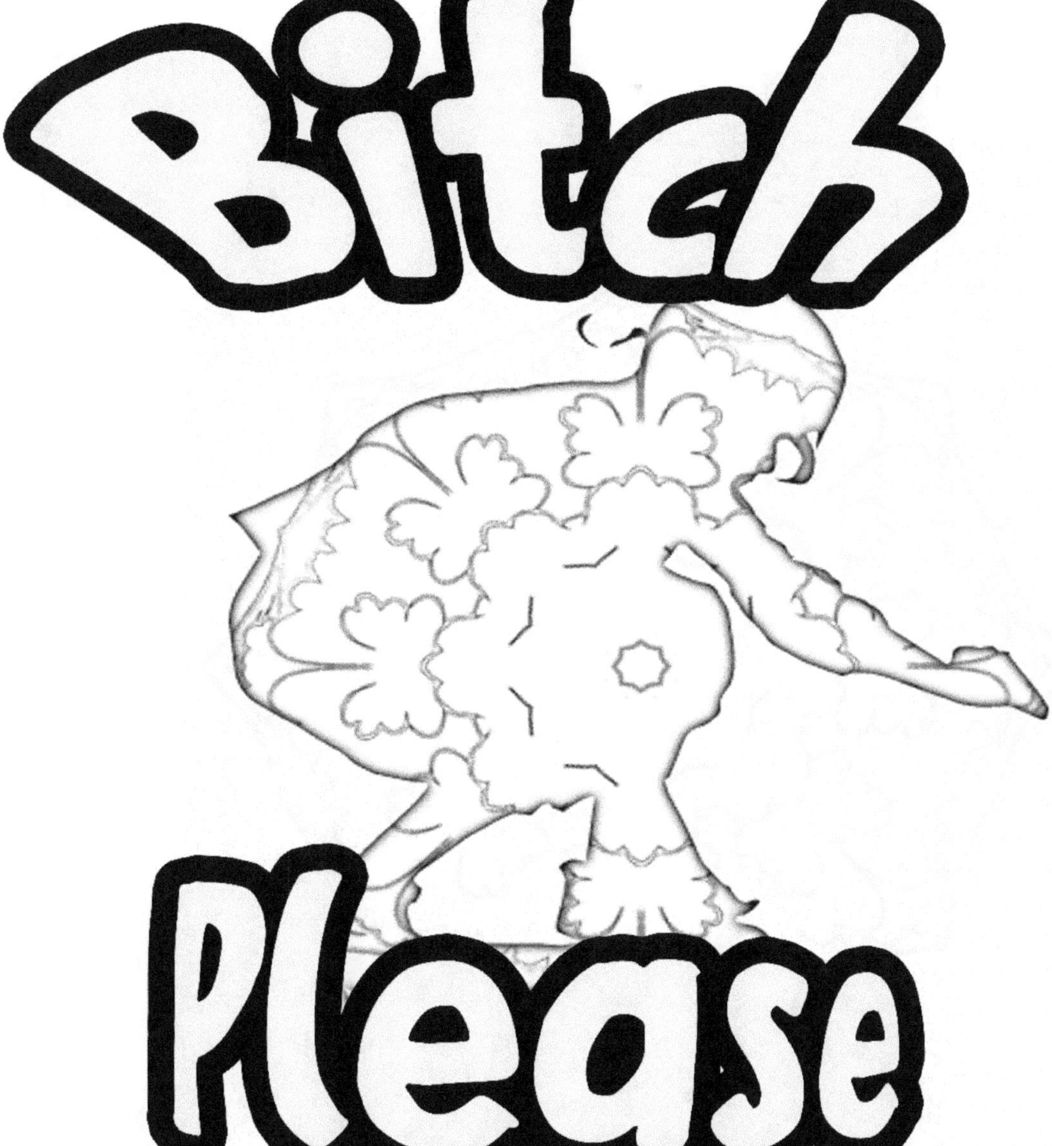
Bitch
Please

# Eat Shit!

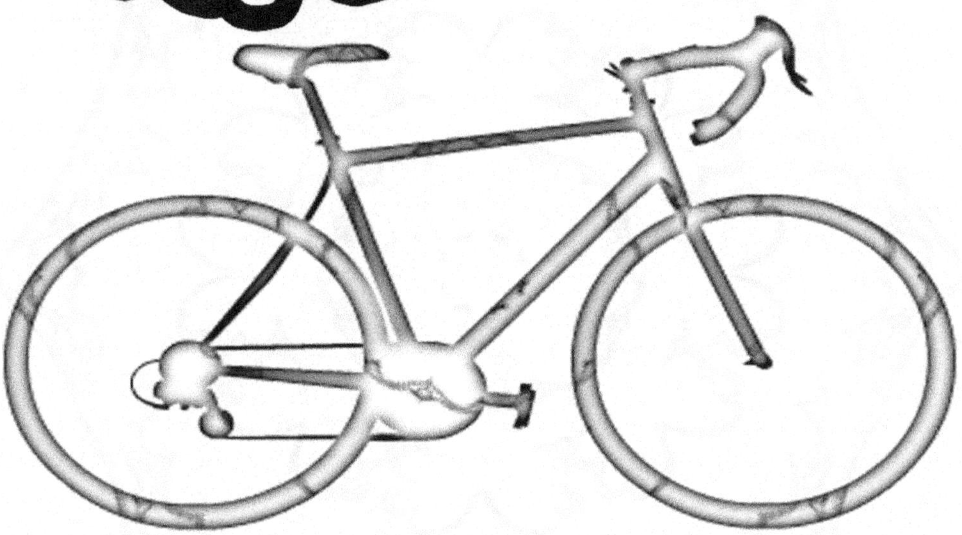

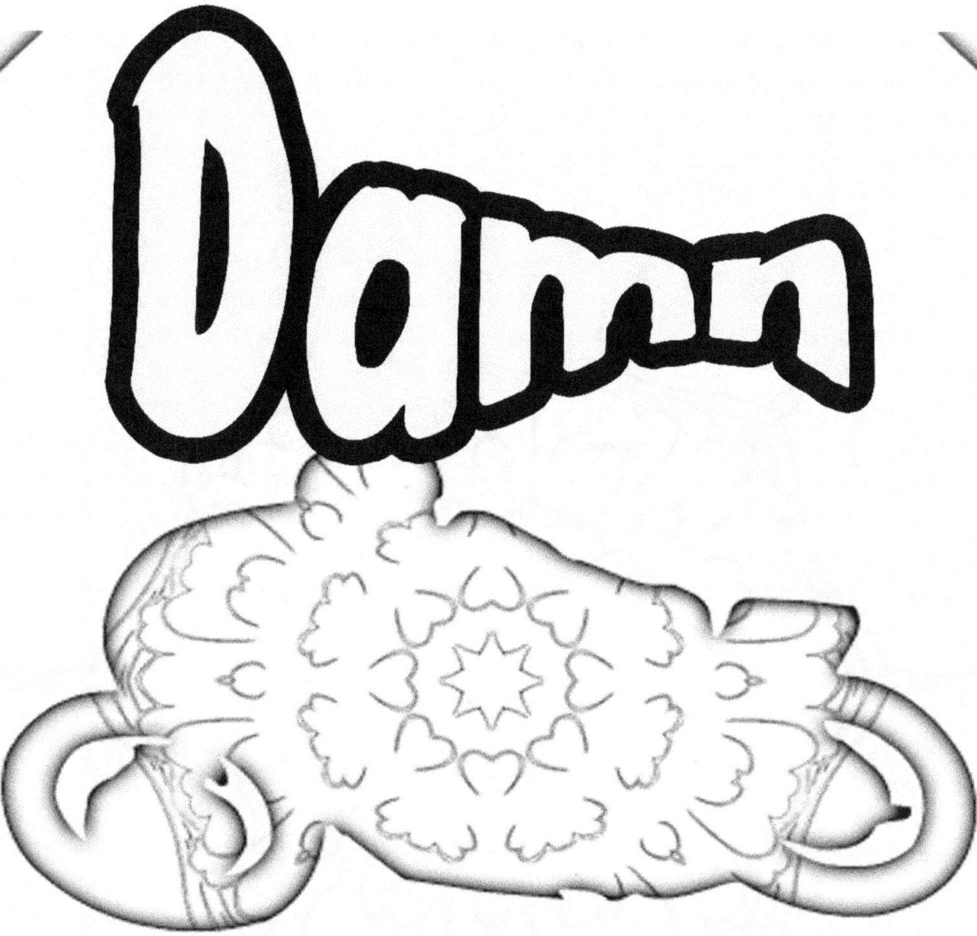
Damn

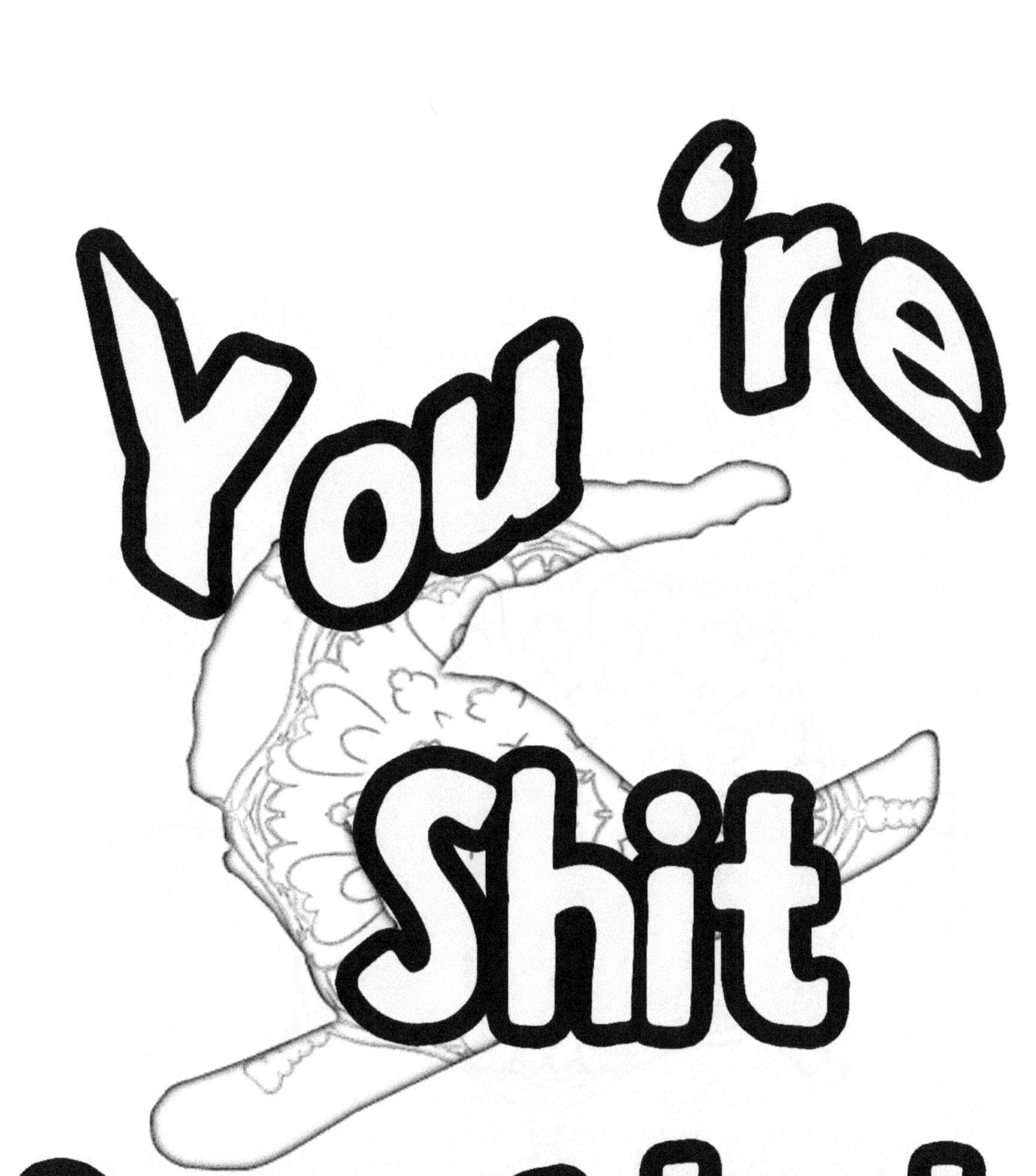
You're
Shit
Out of Luck

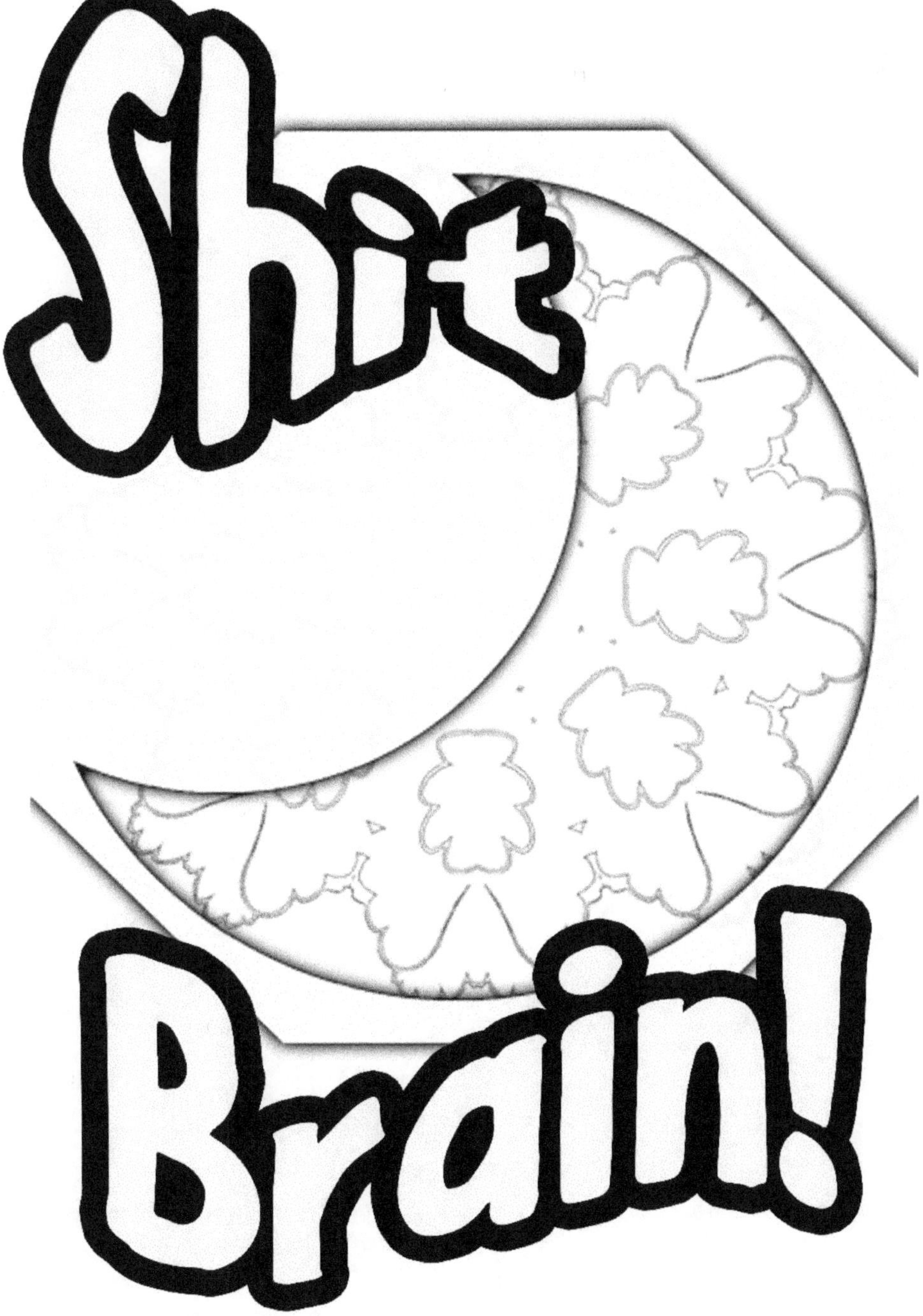
Shit
Brain!

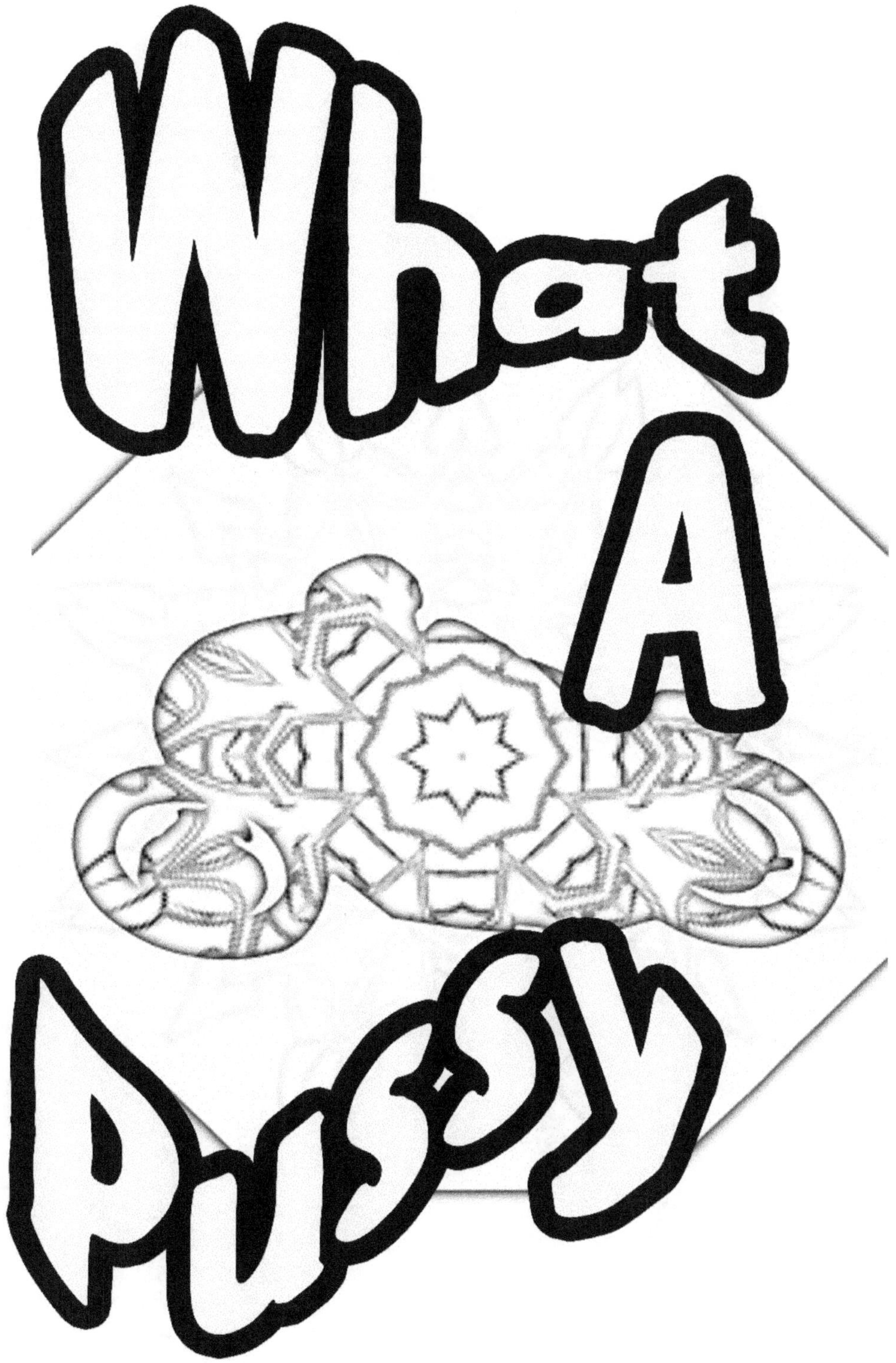
What
A
Pussy

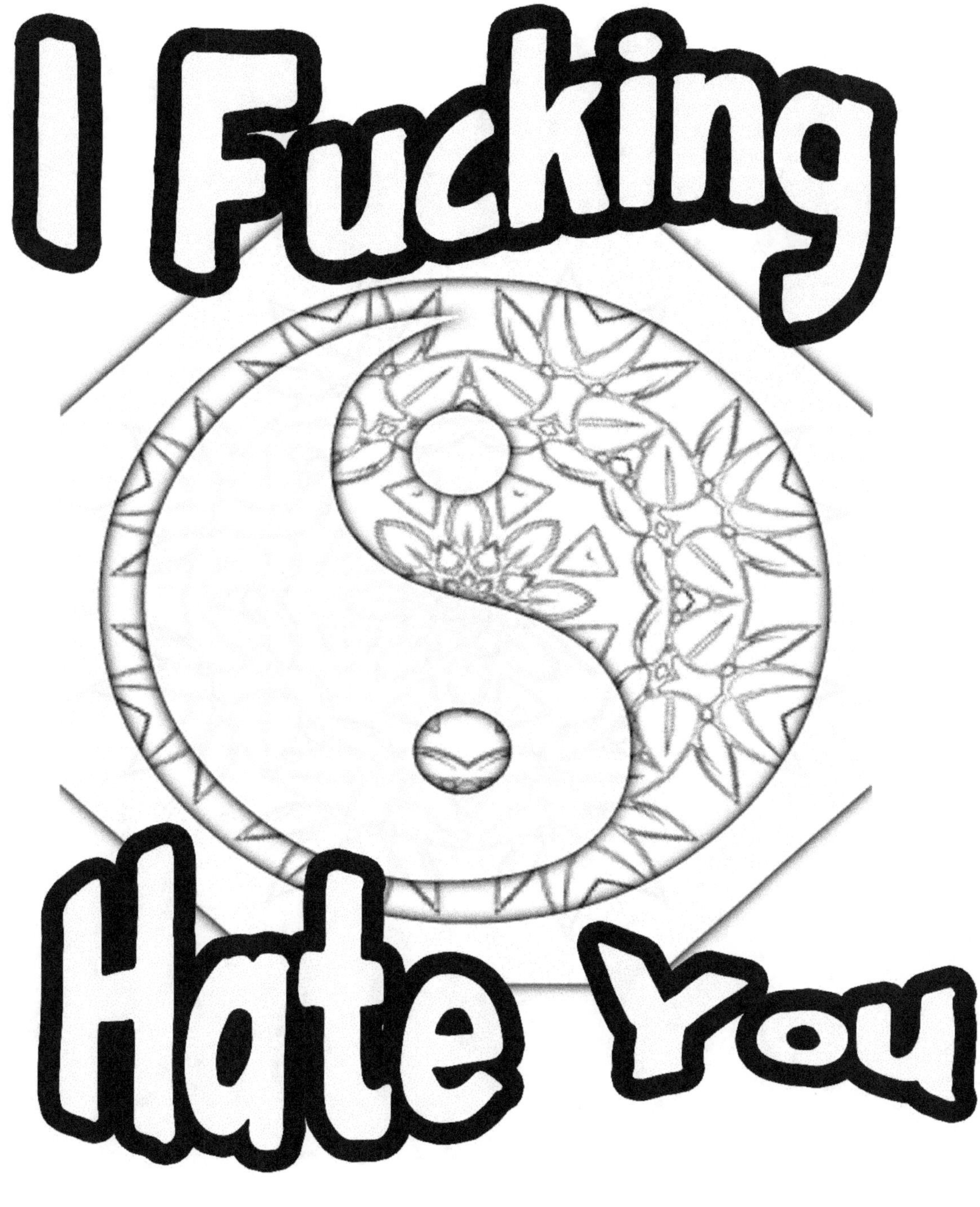
I Fucking
Hate You

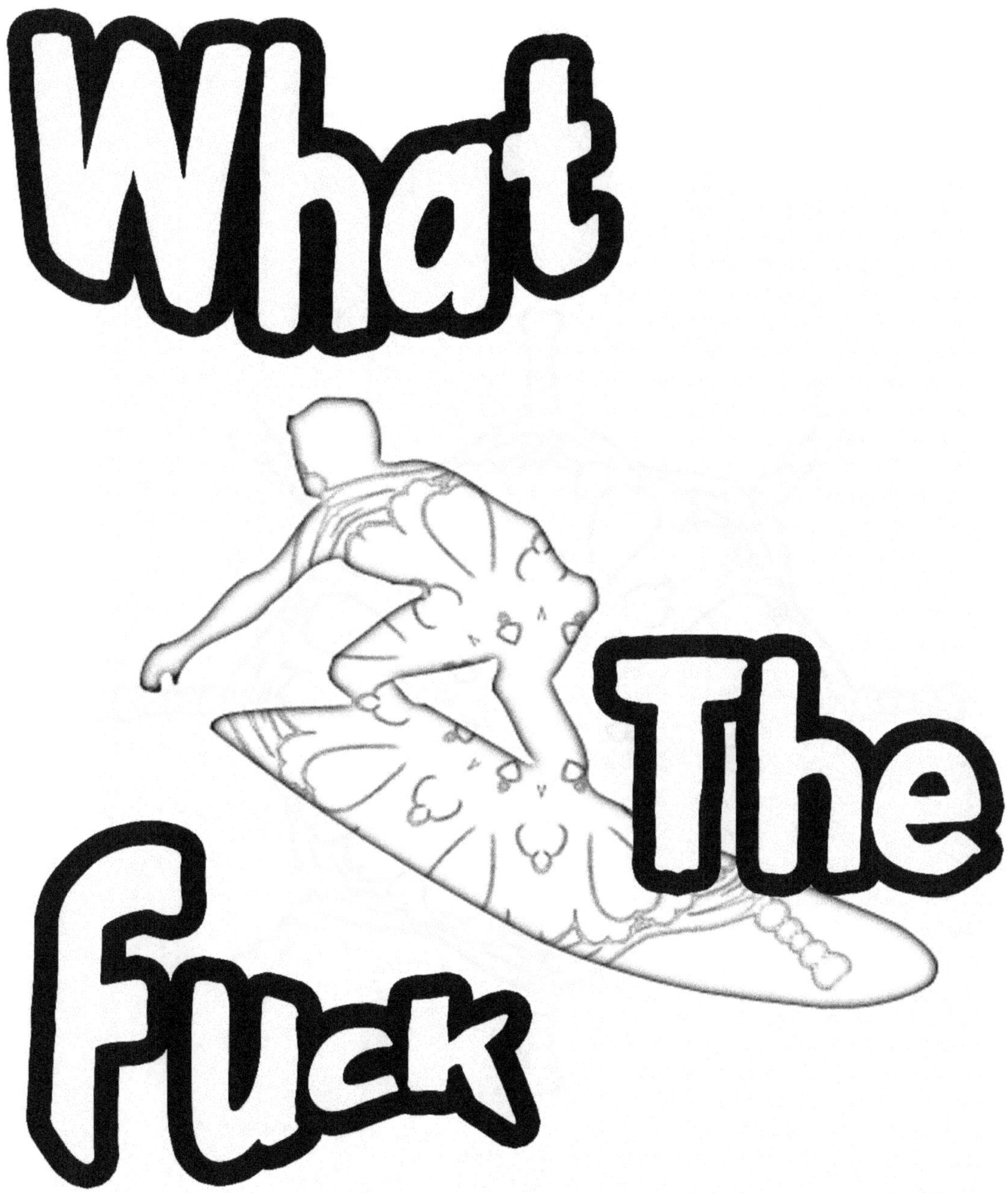
What
The
Fuck

# Son Of

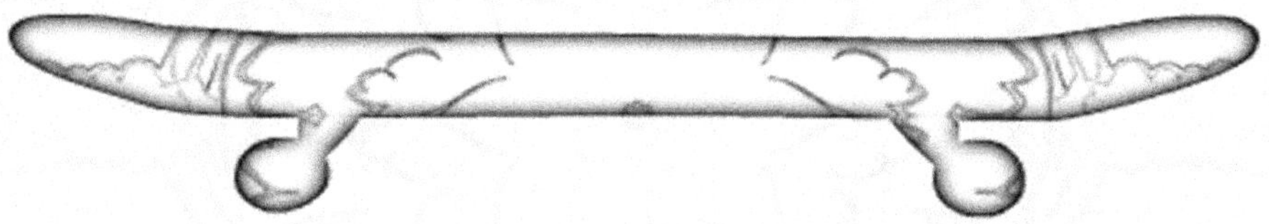

# a Bitch

# Bastard

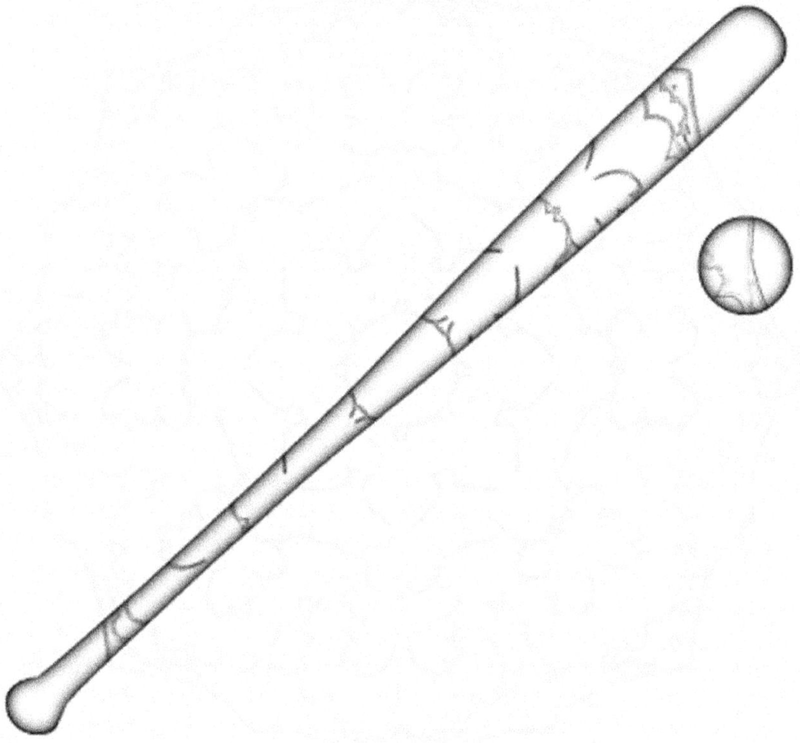

# Jerk

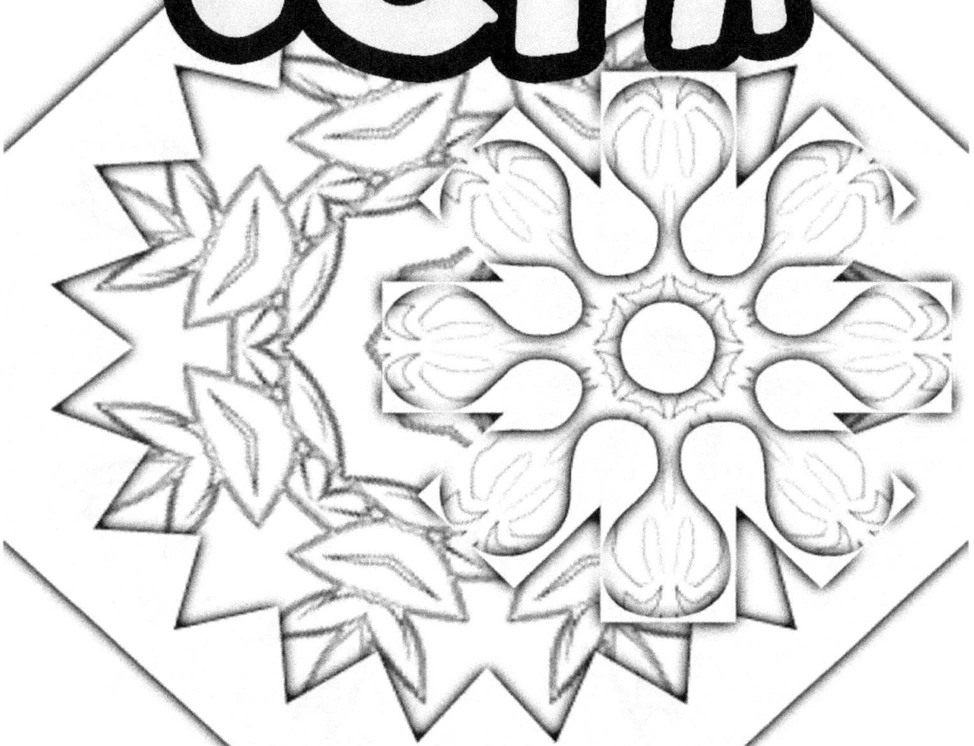

# Note

www.ingramcontent.com/pod-product-compliance
Lightning Source LLC
Chambersburg PA
CBHW080638190526
45169CB00009B/3426
*9781533075338*